I0721028
Plain Cain
Ruth Lee
Well, you didn't know,
and how could you know
with the old world
still so young around you?
and you never meant
to hit that hard
(whoever does?)
but you did and he fell
and the hell on earth
came right up to meet you.
and how to tell Mom
who'd had falls of her own?
how to tell Mom,
who knew evil from good,
that her boys after all
had been boys.

You're invited to follow
Jesus into the wilderness.

visit cpimn.org/immersion

Bathroom Reading for Irregular Christians

In This Issue

Images: Adobe Stock.

Our mascot's name is Hieronymus, Hi for short. He can be reached by email at hi@holyshitjournal.com.

Submit short fiction, poetry, and/or creative nonfiction at holyshit-journal.submittable.com. Submissions are generally open August through October but may be extended, shortened, or completely rescheduled at the editor's whim.

I apologize for Hi's language on page 23. He was a little freaked out. I mean, we all were. I mean, Jesus H. Christ has officially left the popsicle stick, amirite? Hopefully with his sense of humor intact.

There is a monster near the end of this journal. Come to save us all.

Douter

Joshua Gage

My heart is a chapel, illuminated
by votives, each sharpened flame a scar
that, once committed, gutters
in perpetual adoration,
unable to be blown out.
Pilgrims steal beneath my skin
overnight to leave offerings
and build confessionals from wax and smoke.

There are too many fires here;
the weight of so much heat
threatens to scorch the stones.
There are no prayers that I can ache
to keep the conflagration at bay.
Only now, an angel, adorned in moonlight,
thumb and forefinger licked.

Dyspneic Beckoning

Joshua Gage

I wake to evening and a lonely sound—
not a lover's snore nor a clatter of heels,
but still something rhythmic, measured,
some shift of air that draws me forth
through barren rooms to an open window
where an angel perches, hand extended
in invitation. I would tell you
that all is silence, but there are crickets,
frogs, the neighbor's air conditioner,
the night's routine syllables gathered
in organic vesper. Only my lungs
forget the hour and refuse to breathe.

Smudge

Joshua Gage

In the house of my misery,
the angel lives in the basement.
It ascends, always after noon,
unshaven, a cigarette
holstered between its lips,
another behind its ear.
Some hours, I believe it loves
the sandalwood of the cologne
that outlines my shirt collars
more than it loves me.
It strings itself across the couch,
snorts through game shows,
descends before the local news
back to shadows amongst the furnace
and the cat's litter box, remnants
of my screams in its pockets.
It pounds them smooth
against the stones, then braids
them into a throbbing rosary
that it shuffles between yellowed fingertips.
It prays for me, and each word
rallies the clouds to storms
and slices the air wide with singing.
Tomorrow, I will lick the salt
from my lips and taste
where the music lifted.

Courier

J. Bradley

I flip the crab upside down. It didn't sense any of my intentions, just like the last three or four I've done this to. I crouch next to the crab, pin it gently down with one hand as I pull out what I want to write out of my back pocket, along with a Sharpie. I pull off the cap of the Sharpie with my mouth, hold the cap between my teeth as I slide the back of the Sharpie into it.

I look over at the note next to the crab. The sunlight hits it in a way where I can't see what I wrote on it exactly. I can make out "home" and "miss you" but not much else. I was afraid if I wrote on the receipt with a pen, I'd tear the last thing that Ann touched.

I shush the crab as I start to write on its belly. If this doesn't end up on the news, I'm hoping it'll at least pass along the message to all of the other crabs it might run into. I remind the crab before putting it back in the water how I don't have room for all the Anns in the world, just the one.

The Colony

Frank Roger

1

Champagne is flowing freely at the headquarters of the European Space Agency as great news is announced about the agency's biggest project ever.

A spokesman for the agency declares in a live interview on TV: "Ulysses has made a safe landing on the lunar surface and is already transmitting data. The first unmanned European mission to the moon is a success. It is now clear to everyone that Europe is fully taking part in the exploration of space. Americans, Russians, Chinese and Indians now have a serious contender in the game to reckon with. It goes without saying that this is merely the beginning of a grand space adventure for our Agency. Now, some people may be tempted to start dreaming of our first manned mission, but let us focus on the present and start work with the treasure trove of information Ulysses is transmitting."

Not a word is said about the technical problems the mission was facing in the beginning: error messages, news about technical mishaps, predictions of a mission bound to fail. "All's well that ends well," a major newspaper has it, even if the mission has barely started rather than ended.

2

Ulysses has landed where it was supposed to, all its technical systems are functioning properly and it is transmitting data to earth: so much for the good news.

There is some uncertainty, however, concerning the problems that arose right after the launch. Now that we are told the lunar module's first images cannot or may not be shown to an impatient audience, the grapevine has been stirred into action. The Agency's spokesman denies there are any serious problems and promises that images will be shown "as soon as some issues have been dealt with." He cannot elaborate on the nature of these issues.

The media abound with speculation as to what may be going on.

3

Images supposedly taken by Ulysses were leaked on the internet by a staff member of the European Space Agency. The images are of poor quality and seem to show signs of activity. It is impossible to determine whether the footage is genuine, edited, or simply fake. A few hours later, social media are teeming with comments, and later that day the ESA makes an official announcement.

"The video images transmitted by Ulysses show irregularities that are related to the technical problems the mission was facing after the launch. We are now examining the nature of these problems and will take appropriate measures."

The rumors, spread by anonymous sources, that stowaways have sneaked aboard Ulysses are adamantly discarded by the spokesman: "These rumors are sensationalist nonsense. Security measures at Corou spaceport are very strict. Moreover, there is no room for stowaways aboard the lunar module or the booster. In the unlikely event of a human being or an animal going along for the ride, it would inexorably end in death: the acceleration, the lack of oxygen and temperatures well below zero will not leave any living creature a chance."

4

Expectations are high as the ESA announces a press conference after more images were leaked, unmistakably featuring moving human figures. The spokesman breaking the news is clearly ill at ease:

"We can now confirm that prior to the launch of Ulysses, unauthorized persons managed to gain access to the restricted area as well as to the lunar module itself. Although all scientists and experts explicitly exclude the possibility of surviving the journey from the earth to the moon without proper facilities, these persons apparently beat the odds. Nothing is known about their identity, their motives or their methods. When our investigation sheds light on this mystery, we will provide further information. Finally, I am happy to report that this problem does not seem to interfere with Ulysses' regular activities. The lunar module keeps transmitting data and has started its soil research program."

Earlier attempts by desperate refugees who miraculously survived a flight, hidden in an aircraft's landing gear, are recalled in the media. Everyone realizes, however, that there is a world of difference between air travel and a journey through the void.

5

The BBC broadcasts an interview with a Somali man, who prefers to remain anonymous, and who claims to be the brother of one of the stowaways who travelled to the moon with Ulysses.

"My brother and his wife prepared their trip thoroughly," he says. "They did not arrive at their destination alive by coincidence. They trained in cold storage rooms and underwater, building up resistance to temperatures below zero and the void. They manufactured thermal suits made out of discarded insulating material, and multi-layered plastic bags with an oxygen supply. They also smuggled food and water aboard, as well as some other useful stuff. I'm happy to see that my brother left the entire scientific world awe-stricken with his determination, persistence, and resilience."

Experts and ESA staff members refuse to believe the man's bold claims but cannot give an alternative explanation for the stowaways' accomplishment. "Our investigation is making progress and will eventually allow us to unlock this mystery," the spokesman concludes.

6

The ESA finally releases video footage clearly showing two human figures clumsily moving about on the lunar surface, wearing spacesuits that were crudely stitched together but which appear to hold up well. It is not clear what they are doing, as they are mainly active beyond the camera's visual range.

Some commentators doubt the images are genuine, but ESA confirms their authenticity. "It's a miracle this couple arrived alive on the moon," says the spokesman, "but we have to realize that their chances at survival are about zero. Very soon they will run out of oxygen, food and water, and there's no way to get new supplies up there. Then there are the extreme differences in temperature and the low gravity. We fear this success story will soon come to an end."

The trials and tribulations of the Somali moondwellers are all over the international media. No one is paying attention to Ulysses' real mission anymore.

7

Somali communities of various countries have created a benefit fund for New Mogadishu, as they call their "first extraterrestrial colony," a bridgehead of hope for a people left to its own devices. "Refugees from areas plagued by war, chaos, and famine aren't welcome anywhere anymore, and all host countries claim to have reached or exceeded their immigration quota. The only option left is to push the boundaries and explore new horizons, to go where one is still welcome, where one cannot be sent back, where one can build a future undisturbed, even if theoretically impossible. Time will tell."

8

More sensational news about the lunar expedition is released upon an unsuspecting world: it is now revealed that the Somali woman who made the journey is heavily pregnant. This clearly shows on recent images released by the ESA, and the fact is also confirmed by the alleged brother of the male stowaway (reputed father of the child). He even adds that this is all part of a grand plan, soon to unfold before the eyes of "those who stayed behind" (i.e., the people on earth).

It is now easier to see what the couple are doing on the lunar surface, after the man pushed one of the cameras in another angle. Next to the lunar module, a modest construction is arising, made out of material either smuggled aboard or taken from the module itself. A green mass can be seen under a transparent piece of plastic or glass.

There are plenty of rumors buzzing about in the media. Are those two people building a small moon base? And what could that green mass be? Some claim it's algae or other plants that produce oxygen and can also be eaten. Is this the first step towards a hydroponic garden that will support the basic needs of the "colonists"? Is there a future beckoning then for these two people, where no life was considered possible?

The news of the birth of a child on the moon — the first human child ever not born on earth in the history of mankind — leaves the world stunned and elicits a lot of reactions.

There are some who criticize the parents because it's irresponsible to have a child in an environment that's hostile to life, and where a boy — in the unlikely event of his making it through his first days — is doomed to grow up without friends of his own age, completely cut off from his world and with an unending fight for survival as his only perspective.

Scientists who say it will be interesting to see what influence the low gravity will have on the child's development get all sorts of reproaches hurled at them — for instance for being out of sync with the real world.

According to the father's brother (the child's uncle), by now self-appointed "ambassador of New Mogadishu on Earth," this birth gives a new impetus to the story: "A first step has been taken towards a flourishing, viable colony, a beacon of hope for all refugees in the world."

On spaceports in the United States and elsewhere, security measures and surveillance are upgraded. There are well-founded fears that the Somali success story will set an example and incite other refugees to try to sneak aboard spacecraft.

Refugee communities are cheering and celebrating: the impossible has now become feasible, dreams may come true, a new and unexpected horizon is beckoning. The picture of the father proudly holding up his newborn child (wearing a cute space suit that was obviously made beforehand) in front of Ulysses' camera is without a doubt the most shared image ever.

Flying Out of Charlotte, I Think of Saint Joseph of Copertino

Jim Zola

They called Joseph the Gaper, a childhood taunt,
as he sat and stared. Yelling, beating, pinching,
burning, piercing by needles wouldn't break
his ecstasy brought on by a church bell,
a musical note, God's name. They say
he could smell the stench of sin, that he brought a flock
of sheep struck dead by giant hailstones back to life.

Here he would be just one of the ignored.
I stare into the faces of those who rush from gate
to gate. He could float for hours on the wings
of faith. When a voice calls my number, I rise.

Contented Belly-Crawl

Catherine Zickgraf

Genesis implies the serpent first appeared
in the Garden of Eden with hips, knees, and feet.
But then God cursed it to belly-crawl,
stripping off its limbs as punishment
for Satan possessing it,
crawling into its body to trick humanity,
locking snake eyes ultimately
with God in the garden standoff.

It wasn't the animal's fault.
Lucifer's handoff of the body
back to its owner
came with a curse from their Creator
who said to the serpent:

> *You will be hated now*
> *hidden in the grasses*
> *your slick slice through the dust*
> *will disgust the human masses.*
>
> *Twisting around your brother now,*
> *food your motivation.*
> *And you will remind my humans*
> *how Satan whispers still temptations*
> *to lure them into lust*
> *and lay them in the grave —*
> *because sin is sexy.*
>
> *So your tail will flagellate like sperm*
> *the female body craves.*

Thus, God punished Satan's first victim —
this hijacked animal
the devil's vessel —
possessed for an evil project.

But how fair of God to settle the score
by forcing the innocent serpent
to belly crawl forevermore?

I know that God is just.
I just don't understand His ways.
Genesis says that although sin cursed the Earth,
God would send His Son to save.

But if I were a squirmy reptile
expelled thin and limbless
through my mother's bowels,
would I resent this dragging my
underside through the dust?

If I were a scaly *culebra*
winding my way through the world,
would I be pissed I was wrongly punished?

No. Because God grants creation adaptation.

If I were the snake,
I too would be granted
rows of scales like fingernails
to unshock my journey over the gravel,
I too would be given
the gift of skin-shedding —
the ability to undress down to fresh keratin,
leaving a delicate sock hanging
over the bark of tree limbs.

If that were me,
I would belly-crawl contentedly.
I would slither and crawl as my lot in life,
because not questioning why I slither —
but simply slithering —
would be the highest purpose of my existence.

Fall from Heaven

Catherine Zickgraf

I landed on his patio tile, wild from my travels
but ready to shine my soiled down
and align my feathers toward the next little town.

He was more afraid of me than I was of him.
But he was kind, and I became his precious wife.
Still I'd fly across the broad sky,
soaring out of his sight.
Then he'd fold me back into his chest at night.

He was my trunk, my tower,
holding me with the power
of a thousand branches of light.

He'd watch me folding laundry.
I was his wide-eyed angel,
but my heart ran away through the curtains
toward the puddles of rain.

Some of you carry the same secret:
you long for other lives.
Many have hurt their lovers this way,
rowing, rowing, but only stirring the dirt.

I assumed he'd realize with time
I couldn't be his Gentle one
or the pure soul he vined
his arms around at night.

So I'd sleep beside him afraid
of when the sweetness behind his eyes would fade
and change to a fire and rise up to scorch me —
charring my wings into shards,
fingers, feet, and feathers marred.

I imagined my wings scarred
and bent around me on the floor
and wondered if I'd have to scratch a path
under a closet door.

These were my fears, yet he loved me with tears
though I'd escape that love and fly away to breathe.
And when I returned with thorns in my toes,
he'd kneel down like Christ to wash my feet.

What do you do with this instinct to fly,
when flying too far can get you lost
and you know if left lost,
you'll turn wild again?

But the weight of the mundane flat-lined my brain.
It's sick to be dissatisfied with golden bracelets,
a glowing hearth, children in bed,
and his smell in the dark.

So I would sleep with these *what ifs*:
what if the next time I flew away,
he told me not to come home,
chased me from my children
and sent me off alone?

Then my God came and changed my instincts
to keep me from losing it all.
He transformed me into a new creature
revealed like the springtime thaw.

They say only screwed-up people need God,
and I say I agree.
The old things don't want to pass away,
and we all fall short in our greed.

So enough of this metaphor,
if I left our bed, I'd get as far as the floor
with no one to love me that strongly again.
I only see him in a room full of men.

Our youngest still needs to cuddle between us
sometimes, though his elbows keep us from rest.
Eighteen years of marriage, not by my power,
it's God's faithfulness that has passed the test.

Just Give Me the Right

CLS Ferguson

Just give me the right words
Just give me the right things to say
Just give me the right expression on my face

Take me by the hand
Lead me to the ballroom floor

Just give me the right moves
Just give me the right posture
Just give me the right embrace

Put your hand against the small of my back
Place your cheek on my cheek

Just give me the right breath
Just give me the right gaze
Just give me the right caress

Another Attempt at a Romance with an Old Flame

CLS Ferguson

A boy I had known in middle school came into the Souplantation. We'd never had a romance — just a bit of sexual tension every time we saw each other. When I brought him a refill of his strawberry lemonade, we exchanged phone numbers. He called later that evening.

What I thought I heard him say: . . . then you make a left on Crow Wing Road. My address is 11011 Palindrome.

What I said in response: Could you spell that?

Him: Fuck no!

Me: "Fuck no" is how you spell 'palindrome'?

Him: I must have missed something.

When I made that left onto Crow Wing (after an arduous set of detours, due to San Diego shutting down some major roads for the evening), there he was, standing on his driveway, on Crow Wing. I approached him and he handed me a salmon/peach colored Post-It note with PALINDROME in black Sharpie. I had an incredibly confused look on my face, I am sure.

Me: I thought you said you lived on Palindrome.

Him: No, I said my address is a palindrome.

Me: Now I get it. You were the one making the smart joke, and I totally missed it.

Him: I thought you were just bein' a bitch, tryin' to see if I knew how to spell it. I guess you thought I was bein' an asshole for not spelling the name of my street!

My text to him, post-visit: 11011 Palindrome. Don't forget the tissues; he swears he's not boyfriend material. (Pun intended.)

Because the aforementioned text was completely un-responded to, yet rich with inside jokes, I can only assume he did not get it (in one sense of the word or another).

Trip to the Grocery Store

CLS Ferguson

"Six lamb shanks please." I stood in front of the beautiful meat display at the grocery store.

"Are you sure you want six? Our shanks are pretty big," was the butcher's response.

Upon looking at the shanks, I agreed with the butcher and revised my order to three. He wrapped my shanks in plastic and paper, and I turned away, sleeping baby on my chest, toward the checkout counter.

The spice aisle was where I saw them. There was something grainy all over the aisle, like sand. It appeared no carts had run over it yet, but there were footprints. Not shoeprints. Footprints. Footprints so well defined that those detectives on Forensic Files would have been thrilled to find them. I was almost disappointed that I had no plaster with me to take a mold.

I continued along the aisle, careful not to slip in the sand or wake the baby. The footprints got larger — went from human adult male to ogre size. The sand became finer and made me sneeze. Other people in the aisle went about their business, pretending to understand the food labels they were poring over and putting far too many calories into their cart. I wanted to shout, "Don't you see these footprints!?" I also didn't want the baby to be disturbed.

As the footprints became larger, and others around me acted as if everything were normal, my wonder and amusement gave way to anger. Where was the manager? Why had this not been cleaned up yet? Whose footprints were these? Was this some sort of stupid prank? I bent my knees and dipped toward the sandy substance, thinking I could prove it was spilt spices. I picked up a few grains on my fingertips. No. Definitely sand.

I eased a little, remembering my childhood in San Diego, those summer days that stretched on for hours from before noon to sunset, my sister and I bobbing in the icy Pacific until our mother insisted we return to shore. We would beg to stay in the water despite our wrinkled fingers and toes, despite our teeth chattering, despite our lips turning blue.

I wiped the sand on my jeans and continued toward checkout. Near the checkout counter, I discovered the source. There it was — a mound of sand. The footprints remained a mystery, however. The purpose of the mound escaped me as well.

The woman at the cash register greeted me, "Sorry about the sand."

"Oh, so you see it, too?" I asked, likely sounding like a dope.

"Of course," she said. She carefully rang up each item, placing a small mound of sand on each one. She put her hands in her pockets to retrieve more sand, so that she had just enough for each thing. "Isn't it beautiful?" she asked me, apparently referring to the sand.

"Honestly, I feel I could do without it," I mumbled.

"Don't say that!" She warned, "or more footprints may appear."

"I think those bags will be too heavy for me to carry with the baby and all," I was reaching for a reason to leave the store emptyhanded.

"Shhh." The cashier appeared genuinely frightened.

I began to walk away, toward the door. The cashier was sweating, shaking, and scaring me now. I picked up my pace. As I rushed toward the sliding glass doors, the sand multiplied and was filling up the store. I sheltered the baby's curls on top of her head from the sand coming from the ceiling. I pulled my keys out of my pocket to have them at the ready.

As I put the baby in her car seat, I felt a tap on my shoulder. It was a police officer. "Were you just shopping in there, ma'am?"

"No, sir." My first lie to a cop.

"Good thing," he responded, "Or I'd have to escort you back in. Once the sand has touched you, you aren't allowed to leave. I only breathed in a little and even I'm stuck in this parking lot."

"I'm sorry to hear that," I commiserated as I slid into the driver seat and started the car. The sliding glass doors were overtaken by sand by now, and the shaking of the earth woke the baby as we made it out of the parking lot toward home.

God & Other Famous People

Elizeya Quate

Ask a true fan to choose between God and Michael Jackson and they won't quite know what you're asking.

What if being a true fan meant that you could feel your specific famous person dying, like the moment that Prince or David Bowie or Michael Jackson died, their 10,000 truest fans woke up in beds around the world and cried and cried and didn't know why?

When I die, I hope my thoughts wake up in their own beds, cheeks sticky with the same flavor of tears. When I'm done crying tonight I go back to sleep or something else that's climax-proof — I wouldn't know a goddamn climax if it jumped up and laid eggs in my rectum. What would those eggs be? Just like on Easter, each egg would be a reincarnated famous person, they'd arise fully formed at the most iconic part of their career, re-exist for exactly seven minutes and then die where they stood. How much would a seven minute reincarnation egg of David Bowie go for on eBay? My guess is low millions USD, but realistically it could be much, *much* higher!

On this affectless morning, all the elastic has gone out of all the window panes. I sit on a folding chair in my dirty jacket with my dirty fingers and pick dead cells from the grease of my eyebrows. Today the rain doesn't seem to know what winter means, and the windows are covered in glass zippers. I like jackets and thermal shells with a greater-than-average number of zippered pockets: they make me feel covered in little sacs of pure potentiality. Footsteps in this chilly season are like pockets: they give you a sense of where someone might go and can be surprisingly difficult to fake. All over the world there are sacred footprints, some of them chiseled into stone or left in mud or in the lowest basins of underground cave networks that are purported to be the footprints of gods, or of holy men, or of powerful spirits. Eve's Footprints in Southeast Africa, or the Sri Pada — a footprint of the Buddha or Shiva or even Adam or even St. Thomas Aquinas. These sacred footprints either fall within the subcategory of ichnofossils — fossilized evidence of biological activity, including footprints — or petrosomaglyphs: carvings that are designed to mimic the evidence of biological activity, such as when footprints of faeries or spirits are carved into living rock. Ichnofossils that may be mistaken for petrosomaglyphs are called mimeoliths; they look like evidence of biological activity but aren't.

When I think about who I'm praying to, I realize that the identity of my savior has become an enigma that I will never solve. I think about famous people, how you can feel the charisma of a really famous person from a great distance. You think about them when they aren't there. You feel their will, hear their voice, are defined (even at a low level) by the intensity of their presence. People who believe in God can often feel close to God, like the way people feel close to David Bowie and Prince and Michael Jackson. It's like being in a long-distance relationship with a person who will never break up with you. There's something obviously appealing about that notion.

Sometimes I wish that I could believe in more things — not necessarily God or America, but some cool idea that I could be in a long-distance relationship with, secure in the understanding that we would always stay together, even long after I've died. That's why God is the ultimate famous person. More people feel close to her than anyone else and she never dies so no one ever has to feel sad about God the way they feel about David Bowie.

You might get the idea from reading this that I'm anti-religious or have other weird axes to grind, but I can't even muster an earnest atheism properly. I probably have about as much respect for the secular worship of money or sex as I do for the religious worship of God or Death: a bit, though more envy than respect. I'd love to *be* money, to *be* sex, or even to *be* Death or God. That way everyone would want a piece of me, but no one would ever quite get enough.

Maybe who I really envy is my fellow humanoids whose belief-muscles are in better shape than mine, or maybe at some deep-down level I really yearn for some X-Explains-It-All! System, which is what initially attracted me first to Marxism, then to anarchism and then to various Left-libertarian blendings of autonomy, abundance, and egalitarianism. But X-Explains-It-All! Systems are more boring to me now than the history of accounting software, so I don't think I'll age into that tendency. People who do age into X-Explains-It-All! Systems are funny. Not in a bad way. It's as if some ideas are like foot calluses or male pattern baldness or little bumps of shiny skin — at a certain age, they just start showing up and you have to make a big effort if you want to get rid of them.

I don't know God personally, but I like to feel close to her. What I do is imagine that God is close by, just hiding under a dead bush or a pile of leaves and the gray rain mists glow a little brighter. I guess I still feel pretty depressed, like the sky weighs 10,000 lbs and my feet are timid jellyfish hoping to one day be fossilized, hoping one day to leave a shimmering mark on something as important as a living rock. This morning God is everywhere: God is my mom and God is the trees and God is the air and God is the breath that crawls out over the nicotine phlegm of my throat and mixes with the general dampness of the day. A great transparency pervades the forest air, as if everything solid is looking for a way to yield its substance toward a world beyond. I can't quite believe in God but sometimes I do feel God so close to me, closer than my skin or the tastebuds of my tongue, closer than my blood or my swollen loins, closer than my desire for cancellation or unconsciousness. Feeling isn't believing — not for me (I wish it was). But that doesn't make this feeling of God anything less than real.

1:1

Larry D. Thacker

When that Ark up in Kentucky goes bankrupt,
what will become of it? Like our strip malls
surrounded by semi-stubborn asphalt, nature

will have a hard go at it while business leaders
knock around some lowball prices for the oddity.
The blacktop will crack. Kudzu will threaten.

Pigeons will roost in all the crannies, claiming
themselves masters of the cobwebbing rafters.
Leaks will find way through the shoddy joints

that would have never survived God's true test.
The gift shop, full of hoodies and bumper stickers,
and Noah bobble heads, will fall into disrepair.

What will the second group of owners morph
the place into? What kind of deal will the state
make with them to unhinge this stinking place

from its first position as national laughing stock?
The prophesy given unto this seer envisions
a second generation existence of the monstrosity

with all the stalls of the first level converted
to flea market sales areas, with the upper stories
provided as section-eight housing opportunities

for the highest bidding county-feared slumlord.
But when the shit really hits the fan, I mean
when the world has fallen all to shit and zombies

are scratching on the doors bolted from inside,
like we're taught the thousands of drowning
would have when Noah sealed the ark's doors

after God's command, I want to be there myself,
like the man in charge would have been, fighting
off the hangers-on while riding a fucking *T. rex*.

Prostate-Yeti

Zoltán Komor

My doc suspects that I might have an asymmetrical prostate, but it turns out the yeti left his footprint in my ass. This is very depressing news — it would be much easier to live with an asymmetrical prostate than with the footprint of the legendary apeman in my butt. But the doc tells me this could be a real breakthrough for cryptozoologists. So we are now pouring plaster in my ass.

The doc just hums when I ask him if there are any health risks involved when it comes to fast-hardening gypsum enemas. Then he can't stop laughing when the white dollop begins to ooze out from my butthole. He tells me: "This is the most fucked up anal creampie that I've ever seen!" Then he clears his throat, and adds: "I'm sorry, anal creampie is a medical term, it refers to the situation when the sperm leaks out of the rectum after anal intercourse."

He doesn't explain what fucked up means, but I'll look it up in a medical dictionary later.

So we wait. And we wait. But the plaster footprint just doesn't want to come out.

The doc stutters: "Geez. There's something wrong. We might have obstructed your bowels or something."

"Are there any health risks involved?"

"I have no clue." He scratches his head. "I need to look up this whole lower digestive system thing on the net. Go home, we'll figure out something. But if you give birth to that apeman footprint, be sure to bring it in."

But I can't. After a few days my belly starts to grow, like I'm pregnant. A nightmare wakes me up at night. In my dream I gave birth to a plaster ape-baby that smells like feet. I try not to worry too much though. But the idea that the doc forgot something keeps buzzing my brain. If I had the footprint where my prostate should have been, where's my real prostate?

After a few days a blurry video appears on the net. Breaking — they captured the legendary apeman in the forest! Serious evidence: the most convincing footage of bigfoot is found.

I watch the video, and I recognize my prostate. It's huge. And maybe a bit asymmetrical, but almost chestnut-shaped, like a healthy one. As mentioned, the footage is quite blurry, but still you can see the slimy, flesh-coloured nodule crawling between the trees — dry leaves stick to its glutinous globular body. It leaves a long ditch behind in the wet forest ground and cryptozoologists are pouring plaster in the trail.

So the apeman hunt begins: and I can only hope the cryptozoologists will suceed, so I can get my prostate back. Most men keep whining about their prostate being in the wrong place, that the designer messed up something when they were manufactured in the heavenly human-factory, because if they want to experience a prostate-orgasm, which is much more powerfull than the average ejaculation, and it decreases the risks of cancer and impotence, they have to fumble inside their assholes. What weeping pussies! At least their prostate isn't roaming the North American woods thousands and thousands of miles away! But I can't think anymore: horrible spasms begin to torture me, and the skin over my swelling belly begins to tear. A mixture of blood and bad-smelling brown liquid starts to ooze out from tiny opening wounds.

The doc calls. He tells me that, according to Wikipedia, the fact that the excrement can't leave my body might cause some problems, but he hasn't found a solution just yet, so he'll call me a few days later.

Next day, the news channels explode with the title: Finally! They caught the legendary apeman!

The proud cryptozoologist just stands there next to the cage, and grins into the camera. I sit on the couch, watching the television and screaming in pain—I can barely see the screen over my swollen belly, where my prostate appears: it growls sadly in a cage, while the cryptozoologist keeps convincing people how harmful the creature is. To prove it, he reaches in between the bars, and taps the side of my giant prostate. His tapping hand makes squelching sounds, and I begin to shake in front of the TV. A strange, hot, vibrating feeling overwhelms me. I get an erection. The reporters and the watching crowd soon join the cryptozoologist: everybody wants to touch my prostate. The creature begins to purr under the curious hands. And I shiver violently under the mixed stimulations: I can scream from the pain that burns in my bowels and shout from the joy that scratches my pleasure center at the same time. And finally, I can't take it anymore: I burn in the flickering brain-lights, like a moth, and my belly rips open with the ejaculation. Blood, semen, and feces splash everywhere in the room. I believe *fucked up* is the correct medical term. The last thing I see in this world is that a firm, white apeman footprint flies out of me and kicks in the TV screen.

Turdmummy

Zoltán Komor

I discover tiny Egyptian pyramids in my stool. I see miniature bronze-skinned slaves on the toilet paper, stuck in my feces. They get all mangled as I wipe my ass; split-up heads and limbs bulge out here and there from the crap. My face turns white as I flush the toilet.

In the afternoon, I visit my doctor, who reacts with skepticism when I tell him that I'm shitting ancient relics.

"I'm sure it's a pinworm infection," he mumbles sourly. "I'll give you a prescription for mebendazole."

"Last month, I visited an Egyptian Exhibition at the museum. Is it possible that I could have caught it there?"

"It's a question of hygiene!" he shrugs. "You can catch something like this anywhere. At public restrooms, swimming pools, and so on." He hands over the paper carefully, taking great caution not to touch me. "I advise you to sterilize everything at home. Because of their eggs, reinfection can easily occur."

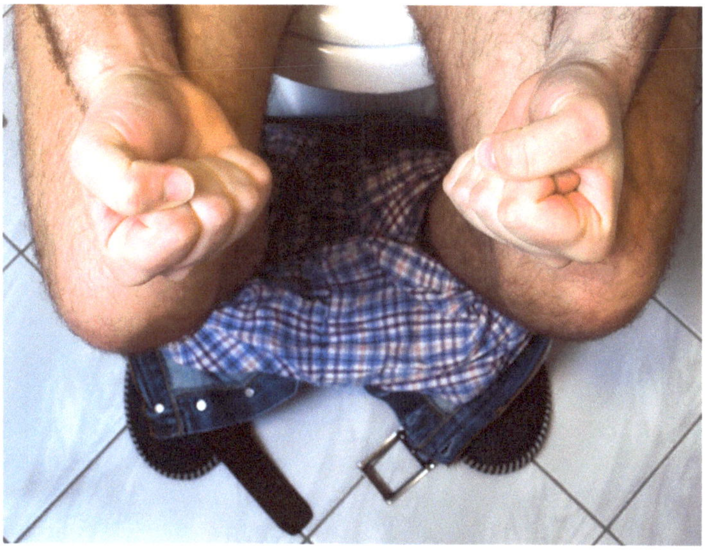

So, I spray disinfectant everywhere. I keep examining the underside of the toilet rim with a magnifier, even though I have no clue what the eggs of the Egyptians really look like — history books don't talk about this stuff.

The instructions for the medicine frighten me — a treatment for several weeks — but I sure want to get rid of my intruders, and much faster than that. Every time I imagine them inside me — carving strange little hieroglyphs into my intestinal wall; removing the brains of their dead ones with small hooks; their priests chanting into my intestinal villi in an unkown language — I begin to feel sick. So I speed up the procedure a bit, and take four mebendazoles at once. I even thrust up a laxative suppository, laughing at the thought that the pale totem of modern medicine will sure scare the little dipshits.

After an hour, I'm sitting on the porcelain throne and whole dynasties explode from my bowels. Some even land on my balls. As I wipe myself, I discover a tiny falcon-headed man hanging down from one of my scrotum hairs. Horus, if I remember correctly from my elementary school studies.

I wipe him down, then I flush the toilet. I imagine myself free, altough I know the war isn't won yet. I take another dose of the medicine and wait.

After a few hours, I can feel that something really large is about to leave my body. It almost takes an hour to give birth to it — I keep sweating and gnashing my teeth — but finally, the mummy slips out. According to the size, it must be a teenager. It's all withered and statue-like, its dark face fossilized in a smile.

My first thought is that it must be valuable. I lay the mummy into my bathtub and snap some photos of it, which I can send later to the private collectors. Then I go to bed. When I fell asleep, nightmares kneel onto my forehead: fecal-zombies in toilet paper strips are chasing me; at dawn, a dog headed man shovels my heart into a bag, like it was just dog shit. Then a scarabaeus rolls away the package.

Waking up, I discover that black abscesses have covered my body. Dark, throbbing blisters. I must have caught some kind of ugly disease from the dead body. In the bathroom, the Fecal-Pharaoh is still enjoying the cold of the porcelain-sarcophagus.

I turn the tap on, but instead of water, gibberish angry chanting pours out from the aqueduct. When in the afternoon locusts get stuck in my DVD player, I realize the mummy is cursed.

I search on the internet. I find out that the only way to break the curse is to return the mummy to its original resting place. So I spend the rest of the day forcing the mummy back into my ass. I use up a whole jar of Vaseline, but still I could only push its head in. I keep sliding it in and out of me to stretch my hole, the royal forehead scours against my prostate.

Later, I feel something split inside of me. By this time, the Pharaoh is in me to its navel, and blood oozes out around it right onto the floor. I imagine myself dying here with the mummy half inside my ass. I'll be its sarcophagus. We're gonna be a beautiful historical matryoshka doll, a real treasure for the museum. We're gonna lie together all silent in the cool gut-corridor of the future, till a higher power explodes us out.

Craphouse Christ Against the Giant Bread Earwig

Zoltán Komor

That morning, the old baker shaped his daughter's sweet face from dough again. Earlier he had used the paste of milk-loaf, but the ants indulged in it, so he now just worked with flour and water. And still, it wasn't perfect, but the old baker knew it never would be: his daughter's lost beauty couldn't be recovered. It had gone like this for months, since the day the miserable girl flayed her own cheek skin.

The baker knew that the ugly earwigs had driven her into madness. They were always around a house — those damned little yellow-black devils — hiding in the cracks of the walls, squirming between the bricks, and at night when darkness descended on the house, climbing out from their hiding places to crawl inside his poor daughter's ears.

First, she started to complain of having nightmares; later, she began talking nonsense, always about the earwigs — that they had forty-times-folded wings hiding under their black scales, and spread them with their forceps-like pincers when they wanted to fly.

"Nasty little worms!" her father growled, not knowing that the girl couldn't hear his words. Her ear canal was blocked by many of these bugs, rubbing their heart-shaped heads to her eardrums, clicking secret insect words to her.

The protruding bones of nightmares scraped the warm body of the night . . . the old baker couldn't forget that horrible summer evening. A storm was coming, but it wasn't the rising wind that had awoken him. Someone was walking in the court.

He snuck out, holding an axe to scare the thief away, and found his daughter standing with her back to him, all naked in the oozing light of the moon, her white skin almost gleaming in the dark. Old pruning shears glinted between her fingers, dark, soggy fluid dripping from its blades.

And then the girl turned to face her father, and the storm clouds scudded from the scream of the old baker. Pieces of slashed skin, short bloody strips dangled from her skull like the whiskers of catfish around her mouth, fluttering in the wind.

"Look, father, I unfolded my wings with my pincers!" she mumbled, holding the messy hand pruners forward, trying to smile with her skull-face. "Now, I can fly!"

Then she fainted, and an army of earwigs rushed out from her ears, running back to the womb-dark cracks of the night on their needle legs.

Since then, the baker has shaped his daughter's sweet face from flour and water every morning. He places the dough-skin on the skull and kisses it. His lips always leave two tiny pits on the girl's new face. But the masks only last for one day; the paste dries fast, it congeals and cracks and hungry mice carry away the fallen-out pieces.

• • •

The father wishes he could see his daughter again sitting in the garden, but of course the birds would notice her, and they would carry away her bread-face. But seemingly the girl doesn't mind staying in the house.

She lives in her darkened room, hiding under the bed, calling her dear earwigs from time to time. The old baker stands guard before her door, his sharp gaze scanning the floor, trampling every six-legged intruder. He pushes tasty fresh milk-loafs into the room under the door. His girl squirms out from under the bed and begins to push the hot sweet paste pieces into the mouth-hole in her pale bread-mask. While eating, she whispers: "All people hide wings beneath their faces, father. We must unfold them, so we can be free! Let the insects come to me!"

But she can already hear a sharp cracking sound, as a running earwig explodes under her fathers unmerciful shoe, and she begins to cry and scream, scratching her bread-face . . . her fingers dig deep pits into the paste-skin . . . she crawls back under the bed on all fours, back to her beautiful crack, and she covers her ears with her hands.

Yet still, she hears the crackings of the dying bugs. She then pinches out two bread-pellets from her face and plugs them into her ears. And suddenly, great silence reigns. Her eyelids get heavy too, so between the bottom of the bed and the cold ground, she unfolds her forty times folded dreams.

After a few hours, she wakes to a strange sensation — something is moving inside both of her ears. The ear canals stretch as the bread-pellets come alive and begin to crawl out. When they push themselves out and fall on the floor, the girl's mouth drops open. Two earwigs squirm their flour-paste bodies, their tiny legs draw unknown signs into the dust on the ground. For a while, the bugs just keep twirling their little heads, then they start to run and disappear in a crack in the wall.

The girl's heart begins to beat faster. Immediately, she pinches out two new crumb-pellets from her face and plugs them into her ears. Smoke flies out from her head as she bakes the new insects. The bread crust hardens into exoskeletons, the tiny paste legs begin to scratch, and the night dries.

The next morning, the old baker arrives, a freshly

kneaded bread-mask wobbling between his fingers. He grabs the beautiful legs and pulls his daughter out from under the bed, like he was just taking out bread from the furnace.

He's about to wrap the skull in paste, but his jaws drop from the sight: the face of his daughter is already covered with bread pellets, and they are moving and shaking, scratching each other with their tiny insect legs—so many earwigs made of bread—and then his daughter's eyes spring open and she mumbles, "We're gonna be free at last, father!"

The old man drops the new mask on the floor; the yellow paste-face hits the ground with a squelchy sound. Then it opens its mouth and starts to sing: "Finally, we can fly father! Up, up in the air!"

And the pale little earwigs jump off the girl's skull and begin to crawl towards the baker. As the pallid little devils march, they clog together to form a much bigger earwig. The buttonholes of madness, the shaking rails of screams . . . now a loaf-sized earwig runs toward the old baker; it jumps into the man's face, its hard pincers tear up the baker's sorrow-wrinkled skin.

Blood splashes onto the wall as the bread bug clutches the man's throat with its peaky legs. It pulls out wings from the baker's head-wound. Behind the torn up skin, membranous film protrudes out, soft as grease-proof paper.

It begins to stretch and tremble, combing the room's stale air, and the old baker emerges, his head tilted way back as the insect wings begin to flap. A strange gurgling sound and blood rise from his throat.

"You're so beautiful, father!" The faceless girl claps her hands, as the old man flies from one corner to another. "Let's liberate the village!"

So they run — to bake new breads.

Together, father and daughter build the giant earwig. The beast is almost twenty-five feet long; on his round abdomen, two giant kiflis, salty crescent-shaped yeast rolls, clatter together, it twirls his enormous heart shaped head. The skull-faced girl jumps to its cracked back and shows the way with a peel. At their side, her father flies, clapping his face-wings, holding a basket in his hands. He throws fresh loaves into the chimneys. The breads in the house begin to shake, then hatch like eggs, and tiny earwigs flounce out to crawl inside sleepers' ears.

The insects' whispering drives a mother into madness: she wakes up and grabs a sharp kitchen knife. Then she flays her children's, her husband's, and finally her own face, kneads them in the bowl with some flour using her hands, making bread which she puts into the oven.

The family sits down to the table with rumbling stomachs, and the bread made of faces begins to sing about freedom. Empty-eyed shepherd boys wander in the streets of the village, attacking and chewing down every face they come across. Regurgitated filmy wings touch the cool air of the night. A young boy rushes into his parents' room naked and on all fours with pruning shears in his ass. The tools keep clashing as his asshole opens and widens. He carves out the flaunting tear-coloured flag of freedom from his parents' heads, cums drops of watery flour onto the floor which clog together to form tiny bugs.

"Let the insects come to me!"

And there they are now, fluttering around the steeple of the church — the flayed-faced angels, in the dark ear canal of the night, pressing themselves to its eardrums. And the giant bread earwig beast crawls up on the building — up, up, and up, toward the moon. It holds its clashing kifli-pincers at the sky, ready to unfold a forty-times-folded God from the clouds.

• • •

Soon, the teenaged son of the priest gets wind of this shitstorm. As usual, he's locked himself into the old wooden craphouse in the yard with some cutout photos of naked women in the afternoon; after the jerking session, the sleep overtook him. But as the church begins to crackle, his eyes spring out.

He looks out in the leaks of the old board toilet house and sees a giant earwig squirming on the house of worship. This makes him spit. He knows these tiny little scum—the shithouse is always full of them. He was killing them all summer, trampling them, hitting them with porn magazines, even impaling a few onto toothpicks, watching their legs kick the air as they died.

He rushes into the parsonage to wake his papa, thinking that he will sure kick the egg-shitting devil's ass. There stands his father, all dressed in soutane, but his head is one giant wound. He holds his own frayed face between his fingers, shaking the bloody skin-rag, yelling: "Eat this! It's the flesh and blood of Christ!"

Bugs drop steadily from his ears.

"The sky shitted in our necks . . . this goes beyond a joke!" the kid screams. He runs out of the house to the yard, picks up a garden hoe and kills his dad with it. He then grabs an empty wine bottle, and sneaks into the cracking church to steal some holy water.

Faceless villagers kneel in the pews, buzzing their insect-prayers into the air. When the boy arrives, they turn their heads toward him and barf up their wings. They fly like torpedos, their stretched-out arms trying to tear down the boy's face, but he begins to spin around with the hoe in his hands, cutting their throats. Blood splashes onto the statue of the blessed virgin, who begins to smile and fart rosy clouds.

The boy keeps hitting the motionless bodies for a while, then runs to the holy water container and fills the bottle with the liquid. He rushes out to bless the wooden craphouse: this will surely warn away the devils from his hiding place. The boy waters the building all around; a few drops even fall on the photos of the naked women who immediately grow out two white wings and shiny glories around their heads.

The kid locks himself into the holy toilet, but as soon as he takes his place on the boards, the building begins to shake . . . it emerges from the ground as it grows wooden legs and hands . . . four giant crosses with the Messiah's sculpture on them. Even a head grows out through the top of the shithouse — the bearded face of the savior.

"Now this is something!" the boy whistles. He pulls down his pants and, moving back and forth the erect joystick between his legs, begins to control the enormous construction.

The wooden shithouse-robot marches towards the giant bread earwig biting the lightning rod on the top of the church. The Craphouse-Christ tramples a few villagers who are clashing the pruning shears in their asses . . . their bodies explode under the robot's stringy passion-legs like clusters of grapes. This makes the skull-headed girl scream on the back of the bread earwigs. She points at the craphouse with her frightful baker peel.

The head-winged insect-zombies gather around Christ, but the giant wooden robot swats them like mosquitoes.

The son of the priest peeps out in the leaks of the shithouse, and when he sees that the daughter of the baker is all naked, his hand begins to move faster—what a beauty — he's already touching her boobs in his head — if only her face weren't so ugly. . . . But then the toilet shakes, as the giant bread earwig rushes at the shithouse, clashing its hard kifli-pincers. The insect legs scratch the putrefying wood, but the Craphouse-Christ beats a hole in the beast's crust-armor and starts to tear out pale bread-crumbs.

The wings of the naked girl quiver. She flies off the earwig and begins to beat the door of the shithouse with the peel.

The boy watches the girl's swaying breasts and he can't resist opening the door for her. But when he looks into the ugly face, into the bony hole, into that neverending black pit, disgust overcomes the lust.

"Please, oh, you dear boy, let me in, so I can play with that wonderful tool of yours!" wheedles the girl. (The wings vibrate her vocal cords.) Suddenly, the boy can feel a strange warmth in his groins, as if the holy spirit has moved into his testicles; he can feel the good will bubbling up inside him. The holes of the glories turn wet. He unhooks and opens the cracking door of the old shithouse.

"Come here, pretty girl!"

The boy with the pulled-down pants winks at the baker's daughter, who screams at him, lifting the peel high in the air to swat the jerking kid. But then the boy's dick begins to spurt out holy water. As the drops fly, the air lightens around them. They land on the girl's transparent, fragile wings. In a second, the holy liquid burns holes into the membrane and the girl begins to fall; her scream draws a chalk-line on the dark air.

The baker peel spears her soft body. The boy watches her squirming like a bug on a toothpick. She pukes out her soul into the church's yard. Meanwhile, the latrine Messiah tears the remains of the giant earwig into tiny pieces, filling the teeth holes of the sky with them.

The last remaining insect-zombies explode under the wooden cross-legs, their blood paints the rising sun red.

The grout of the light hardens in the dark cracks. The drinking-trough of the nightmares is dry. There sits the boy now, watching the impaled girl in the morning glaze, and his heart becomes heavy.

He pulls her down from the peel and lays her on the ground. Suddenly, chirping fills the air as birds arrive, sparrows and pigeons. The boy backs away as the animals engulf the dead. Opening wide their beaks, each one regurgitates a bread crumb onto the girl's skull. Soon the pieces covers the head, masking the bone, and welding together they turn into a face.

The feathery little animals spring into the air and disappear in the line of the horizon. The priest's son stands there, admiring the girl—her soft faceline and insoluble nakedness.

He doesn't know how to unfold this so-many-times-folded beauty with his eyes. He backs away again. And locks himself into the old wooden shithouse.

Muse

Janette Schafer

It was a place of surrender, obsequious
as blown hair is to a gagging wind,
a mezzo voice and a jade sea
drowning me with sound. I was already dead
slipping in it like a jugular wound.

I choked on the bitter taste of iron
its spikes hurting my teeth.
There was too much beauty
cobalt melting into the jewel
efficient and savage in loveliness
eloquent in its torture.

I sat as if in a cauldron
trapped by the blackened lid
my sight narrowed, effaced
the music melting me in a refiner's fire
the dross falling away like spilled perfume.

Ah, but what a sweet passing —
to be liquefied by melodic vibration,
to grow limp like the little death
or a rag-doll hanging from a clothesline,
the words of Lawrence echoing
th' art lovely, th' art lovely.

To a Lost Journal

Janette Schafer

My Pakistani lover was recalled
and lost again even as
his curried mouth blazed
and retreated on my
sickly white skin;
the red barn where we made love
was burning.

I had travelled down the Mother Road
stumbling on broken cement
and misspent gravel
as weeds grew over eyes
and out of the nostrils
of zombie-like doctors
with their mute nurses as they
listed down grassy hallways.

In one poem, I had become
a statue, moss covered,
anchored to a desk as
my body turned to stone and wood.

I know it's somewhere in this house
beneath a couch,
in a pile of unopened mail,
in a shelf between a Bible and
a dictionary, or perhaps
sentient with my hallucinations
it has vanished
choosing death over existence
because it hurts too much to live.

A Photograph of Lori in January

Janette Schafer

There was enough light reaching
like fingers to touch your face,
embracing the tendrils of scarlet hair
with the grace and familiarity of a lover.

A plume of lavender smoke
dancing in front of one eye
scenting the air
with a clove perfume

wind tipping the hat
just so.

And Lee Speaks

George Donald

i want my reward
and i want it now
and i'm here to tell you all the reasons why
and i'll try to make it so you can understand
and so you won't just believe what you hear
and i was mean
and i lied
and i stole things from people's houses
and i never wanted to learn a regular trade
and i hid things like a rat who loves shiny things
and these were things nobody wanted
and nobody loved
and why else hide them under the towels
and under the linens
and it was because i thought it wasn't fair
and because i wanted
and because i saw what i wanted by some chance
and because i didn't believe
and because that vinegar
and foot wash baptist picture of hell where tears
and snot freeze they used to scare me with
and put bumps in my road was no good
and made me need to even things out
and life is more than a choice of dogbite or gravy
and some had so much like the belsons
and i had so little
and the belsons had 270 acres
and the big white house
and stores
and money changed hands
and at the church too
and like the lady who says praise god
and praise him forever
and who was a teacher
and who wore gloves to count the milk money
and used alcohol to clean up
and the smell
and if money was mammon
and evil
and filth why did she smile
and i kept not understanding
and yes it's true I was born at the farmers drugstore
and it wasn't in front of the counter like the paper
and the news said later but in the back
and it was hard for dell
and royce to get momma back there
and they did
and they busted open a box of ladies hose
and stuffed it in momma's mouth to bite
and later uncle hare said that's how it was
and said momma got real big with me
and her belly
and her butt looked like two dogs fighting in a pillowcase
and uncle hare wasn't there when i came
and pa wasn't there either
and two days earlier pa walked
and walked to flat street
and bought some mad dog
and the last words they heard him say
and it was when he was crossing the street was noble
and true noble
and true
and after that nobody said they saw him
and maybe that was ok with momma
and maybe it was because uncle hare was there too
and uncle hare was momma's younger brother
and she was the oldest of seven
and uncle hare got a scholarship
and when he came home from the citadel i would hear him
and he would give auditions to girls in the next room
and it was always when momma was gone to work at night
and it was his room but I heard it just the same
and i heard the talk go from please please to real low
and i couldn't hear who said please to who
and one time i walked around the house
and i looked in the window
and he looked up
and she looked up
and she was the gal from the auto parts place
and all hare said was git
and next morning momma was home
and uncle hare was paving butter on his toast
and i was like esau he was eating off my plate
and uncle hare was generous
and one Christmas he gave momma a sock filled with buckshot
and it was for her to squeeze when she got mad
and to beat prowlers with just in case
and uncle hare was smart i guess
and one day he said something about the philosopher stone
and so i asked
and she said it was alchemy
and i said what does that mean
and he said it was making chicken salad out of chicken shit
and years went by at least some
and uncle hare worked fixing cars when he was home
and momma worked cleaning houses for the nuns
and it made her happy cause they're married to jesus
and momma wasn't married anymore
and momma said always to be nice
and even when she wore her same coat
and had the same little coinpurse when she was out
and they still looked at her the same when she was at the store
and there wasn't no call for that
and so it makes no difference
and momma got extra help
and it was because mopping floors
and washing windows wasn't enough
and fall then winter came
and all the folks waiting in the county offices smelled like mothballs
and sweat in their wool coats
and hats
and they waited while the furnace ticked on
and off
and the windows steamed
and still that bright cold blue outside
and momma waited with the rest for her foodstamps
and everybody's head turned when they heard shoes scrape
        by the door

and the door would rattle
and jingle again
and all the ladies would slide down one
and say again how they hated the first of the month
and though momma
and uncle hare didn't know it i tried to help
and it was in my own way
and i kept notice on the daley's house two corners down
and it was a real november-looking house
and it had windy trees up close
and some of the windows were painted shut
and some weren't
and i found out which
and this is what i found inside
and it was a still life of life
and there were cloths on the table
and chairs
and no lights in the closets
and still i found the silver coins
and just never doubt me a cheesecloth bag
and besides the coins there were rings in it
and i left the bag
and i filled it full of rocks before I did from the fishtank
and then after i felt i broke through glass
and saw shreds that sparkled everywhere
and i was new
and i was bold like ice in summer
and my mind took pictures of that room
and every room
and as i took
and hid i took the people too
and i owned them their parts
and their silver
and rings
and brooches
and gold cuff links
and god knew too
and when i went through the baptist church again
and the tile baptism pool where i snickered at momma
and at the fake bible scene
and at everybody else on my baptism day
and i found the box
and the cash lots of cash inside the lock
and dog-eared metal
and they didn't do baptisms at the river anymore
and quiet quiet while it all goes on
and heave in the dark
and shelves spread out to me in my sight
and yellow porchlights
and empty driveways
and purses
and tiny mirrors that only show your nose
and i thought it was pretty good for me raised on fever
and spit from hell
and fever
and fever like a swamp
and fever like the rot under windowboards
and fever like a sidewalk in summer
and like gray frost in winter
and fever like every word in my head sass pure sass
and fever like sick fever wishing that voice would stop
and it won't
and the air from the window
and you know it's you screaming
and vomit fever with smear of petroleum
and blame jar fever me lame wanting it off my back
and fever dreaming knowing I was meant to be
and momma home from work to look after me
and not knowing it
and this time there was no other way for me
and I could go on
and on so the voice said
and it lied though a little
and uncle hare saw me coming out of the cardle's house
and i was holding the bag
and he drug me out behind the shed
and scuppernong vines
and beat me till I couldn't see
and my eyes
and my mouth swelled shut
and he
and momma
and the law had their say
and it was decided that I should be sent far away
and it was a place far away from other places
and the woods were thick
and mountains all around
and there were trouble richboys
and law cases like me
and it was reach and grab for food
and shove in the line and up early
and lights out early
and on it went
and more of it
and winter summer fall
and bonfires clanking radiators coal dust
and the drum of hundreds of feet
and voices cracking in the chapel
and in the assembly hall
and life there was running back
and forth the laps in the field
and late for assembly
and some dumber
and some smarter but not like me
and lincolns
and caddies on parents day
and momma didn't come it was far
and i thought lots under the naked sky about things to have
and where to go
and about the bald hills in the winter
and frozen creeks to cross
and red leaves in the ice
and you can't stoop for them as you cross the ice
and they look like candy
and the taste of smoke in the air you cant reach
and the houses on farther up
and i didn't know how much farther
and the dark
and houses back below like the candles in the chapel
and i gave up on running away

and went back before they missed me
and i had to work when i was there
and it was the kitchen
and scraping old paint off the bleachers
and i hated it
and they had this old man to follow me
and check on me
and other untrustworthies like me
and one time i had mopped the floor in the infirmary
and the varsity was there for their urine test
and tetanus shots
and that old man shippit was there
and he was helping the varsity
and keeping an eye on me too
and i was done mopping the floor
and i was outside to sweep the walk
and saw through the window down the hall
and he dropped a whole tray of urine samples
and i started to move
and he saw me looking
and the glass
and pee on the floor
and came after me with the mop
and yelled out the window
and made me mop it up
and i wanted to tell him to mop it up his own self
and well i didn't want trouble
and i mopped while the varsity laughed
and poked me in the shoulder
and i rode it out like that i guess
and it was months
and months more
and in the end they sent me to charleston
and they put me at mrs logan's house on rutledge avenue
and it was like probation
and she had me on chores too
and she always counted the silver twice
and there were other people there too
and some she had to take care of
and law people
and wards of the court like me
and it was a big house
and she rented space in the attic
and in the basement
and kept the back room for herself
and sometimes the place was quiet
and the kitchen clock made noise
and clipped like a big ugly pair of scissor opening
and closing when the minute hand moved
and always warning like
and the youth officer came
and checked every friday
and the leather boots cracking up the front steps
and the doorbell echoing
and finally they talked longer in the kitchen
and one friday another officer in a coat
and tie came too
and said you're going back to your county
and to your momma
and probation steps are over
and i went back
and i guess i failed after all
and when i went back I found old mrs fletcher's house
and she didn't know anybody anymore
and not even the nurse
and the nurse was gone
and the kitchen window was open
and i climbed in over the dishes
and i looked in the drawers
and i heard her snoring in the back bedroom
and i went in to see
and she was sleeping with her eyes open
and lots of pills by the bed
and sleeping with her rings on
and the colors of the stones
and the size i knew they were real
and she was born a belson
and i touched her hand
and she didn't move only snores
and i pulled at the rings
and they didn't move
and i filled up my pockets with things from the night table
and her pill bottle tray
and she didn't move
and i went back into the kitchen for some soap for her fingers
and i found it
and i was going to use it
and i heard two sounds together
and i turned to the nearest one
and she was there with a gun
and i ducked
and she fired staring at the other sound
and caught uncle hare in the forehead
and he was head
and shoulders into the window
and he fell backwards outside
and i dove out too
and it was over the sink
and the dishes
and landed on top of him
and his face was red
and some of it missing
and i got up and ran
and ran in the dark
and into the woods
and then i thought why
and i stood there
and caught my breath
and went back
and he was still lying there
and i pulled him away slow across the road
and far into the trees
and nobody saw
and this was better i thought
and i ran home
and i wondered if old mrs fletcher put the gun away
and went back to bed
and forgot everything
and i went home
and washed up

and when momma came home she didn't ask about hare just yet
and not until the third day
and momma called the law
and did a missing report
and two days later they announced a reward
and i said i'd help
and the town
and the woods were combed sideways
and frontways
and it had rained a lot since
and the drag marks were gone
and the law came again
and asked again
and i mentioned it that hare liked a certain path
and well maybe
and there he was
and they put tape around the scene
and after that they took him
and they asked momma later about arrangements
and she couldn't afford a crypt
and the casket
and so they only brought back a jar
and the ashes
and i thought maybe that was better than styrofoam
and tin foil
and plastic flowers like robs uncle poor man
and i hate you uncle hare
and you're on the shelf
and your girlfriend who sat
and cried
and your other girlfriend who called
and hung up when i answered the phone
and your car your big one
and your hairy chest all ash
and i still have what I dove out the window with
and you know that it was all a gyp
and a lie
and i didn't get a reward
and they said it didn't lead to no arrest
and all that swing in your arm
and your fist when you popped my eye
and jaw are ash
and ashes to dust
and really they're more like coal clinkers
and sand
and it was you made momma cry
and you're there on the shelf by the clock
and now it's getting dark
and i hear a storm coming
and momma's at work
and it's rising
and i can't stand it
and i grab you from the shelf
and i'm out the door
and i'm out down the road
and i'm out in belson's field
and i've got the stuff i stole inside the ashes
and i'm crossing the field
and i'm heading towards the woods
and the road on the other side
and the bus station
and the bus to augusta
and the only thing i see between is the ditch
and i bet it's a wide ditch
and i'm up to the edge
and i stop like I hit a wall
and i could see over but i look down
and i froze in the heat
and lightning lit it up down there jammed in the wet clay
and i saw the cow dead swelled belly
and the nose broken like a shell
and the tongue out
and black
and yellow like rotted squash
and the whip of bobwire round the neck
and the big eyes one out
and the other one nested in the clay
and hide moved with maggots to eat everything but the horns
and the hooves
and the tail half floating in shallow water
and i gagged
and lightning burned the trees
and there was no other way to cousinsville road
and i thought i could not jump over but hop down to the ground
and climb out the other side
and it was a stupid damn jump
and me falling in the air
and the ashes flying
and the jewelry
and land up to my armpits in wet mud and rot
and the ashes hare's ashes swallowed
and their dimples in the mud
and maggots would crawl
and eat
and the eaten
and the quick and it's hard for me to move
and the ash jar sank near the dead smile
and crooked teeth
and i have no way out but to grab the horns
and pull myself over
and my hands went deep into the flesh in the neck
and the head
and in between the ribs
and angry maggots poured
and i climbed over
and i'm covered with ash
and mud
and a net of flies
and now the stink is on me
and now my feet come out of the dead flesh
and now my arms clawing up
and now i fall back once at least
and now i'm out
and now bulbs of clay
and hide fall out of my hair
and now no jewels or cash
and i wipe my face with my hand
and now i stand with a crown of flies
and now i run again
and no reward
and i never went back home.

Contributors

J. Bradley is the author of *The Adventures of Jesus Christ, Boy Detective* (Pelekinesis, 2016) and the Yelp review prose poem collection *Pick How You Will Revise a Memory* (Robocup Press, 2016). He lives at *jbradleywrites.com.*

George Donald is the second son of a minister and grew up in a series of rectories in the Deep South. His work has appeared in print on the West Coast, the South, and the Midwest. He trained in Languages, Vocal Performance, and Legal Writing. He works as a Simultaneous and Consecutive Interpreter in a Large Hospital.

CLS Ferguson, PhD, speaks, signs, acts, publishes, sings, performs, writes, paints, professes, and rarely relaxes. Her portrayal of *The Black Rose in Silence,* which she also co-wrote and produced, earned her a best actress and best film award. Her music video, *Secrets & Lies,* also earned accolades. She is published in numerous academic and literary journals. Her memoir collection, *Soup Stories,* is due out on Portage Press in May, 2017. She and her husband, Rich, are raising their daughter, Evelyn, and their Bernese Mountain Border Collie Mutt, Sadie, in Alhambra, CA. *clsferguson.wix.com/clsferguson*

Joshua Gage is an ornery curmudgeon from Cleveland. His first full-length collection, *breaths,* is available from VanZeno Press. *Intrinsic Night,* a collaborative project he wrote with J. E. Stanley, was published by Sam's Dot Publishing. His most recent collection, *Inhuman: Haiku from the Zombie Apocalypse,* is available on Poet's Haven Press. He is a graduate of the Low Residency MFA Program in Creative Writing at Naropa University. He has a penchant for Pendleton shirts and any poem strong enough to yank the breath out of his lungs.

Zoltán Komor is from Hungary and writes surreal short stories. He has translated some of his works to English, and published in *Caliban Online, Thrice Fiction, The Phantom Drift, Bizarro Central,* etc. He has three short story collections published by Burning Bulb Publishing, Morbid Books, and StrangeHouse Books.

Ruth Lee is a librarian in a small, west Michigan town, mom of three, writer of stuff that occasionally gets published and other stuff that she foists off daily onto Tumblr (iwasjustthinkinggeez). Credits include *The Wittenburg Door, Screamin' Mamas,* and the *Saturday Evening Post.*

Elizeya Quate holds the world record for Longest Unintentional-Looking Dance Move. Previously published in *Joyland, The Huffington Post, The American Prospect, twitter.com,* and elsewhere.

Frank Roger was born in 1957 in Ghent, Belgium. Apart from fiction, he also produces collages and graphic work in a surrealist and satirical tradition. They have appeared in various magazines and books. By now he has a few hundred short stories to his credit, published in more than 40 languages. In 2012, a story collection in English, *The Burning Woman and Other Stories,* was published by *Evertype (evertype.com).* Find out more at *www.frankroger.be.*

Janette Schafer is a 2017 Maenad Fellowship in creative writing awardee from Chatham University. She is a playwright, opera singer, and poet living in Pittsburgh, Pennsylvania. Upcoming and recent publications include: *Eyedrum Periodically, Nasty Women and Bad Hombres, VerseWrights, Zany Zygote Review,* and *B.E. Literary Journal.*

Larry D. Thacker's poetry can be found or is forthcoming in more than ninety publications including *The Still Journal, Poetry South, Tower Poetry Society, Mad River Review, Spillway, The Southern Poetry Anthology, Mojave River Review, Mannequin Haus, Ghost City Press,* and *Jazz Cigarette.* His books include *Mountain Mysteries: The Mystic Traditions of Appalachia* and the poetry books *Voice Hunting* and *Memory Train,* as well as the forthcoming *Drifting in Awe.* Visit his website at: *larrydthacker.com.*

Catherine Zickgraf has performed her poetry in Madrid, San Juan, and three dozen other cities — yet homeschooling her autistic youngest inspires her the most. Her writing has appeared in *Journal of the American Medical Association, [Pank], Victorian Violet Press,* and *The Grief Diaries.* Her chapbook, *Soul Full of Eye,* is forthcoming from Aldrich Press. Find her at *caththegreat.blogspot.com.*

Jim Zola has worked in a warehouse, as a security guard, in a bookstore, as a teacher for Deaf children, as a toy designer for Fisher Price, and currently as a children's librarian. Published in many journals through the years, his publications include a chapbook — *The One Hundred Bones of Weather* (Blue Pitcher Press) — and a full length poetry collection — *What Glorious Possibilities* (Aldrich Press). He currently lives in Greensboro, NC.

www.ingramcontent.com/pod-product-compliance
Lightning Source LLC
Chambersburg PA
CBHW041923180726
48295CB00002B/58

* 9 7 8 1 9 3 9 6 3 6 1 6 4 *